FAR-OUT GUIDE TO THE

Icy Dwarf Planets

Mary Kay Carson

Bailey Books
an imprint of
Enslow Publishers, Inc.
40 Industrial Road
Box 398
Berkeley Heights, NJ 07922
USA
http://www.enslow.com

For Laszlo Lee Thomas

Bailey Books, an imprint of Enslow Publishers, Inc.

Copyright © 2011 by Mary Kay Carson

Library of Congress Cataloging-in-Publication Data

Carson, Mary Kay.
     Far-out guide to the icy dwarf planets / Mary Kay Carson.
        p. cm. — (Far-out guide to the solar system)
     Summary: "Presents information about icy dwarf planets, including fast facts, history, and technology used
to study them"—Provided by publisher.
     Includes bibliographical references and index.
     ISBN 978-0-7660-3187-6 (alk. paper) (Library Ed.)
     ISBN 978-1-59845-190-0 (Paperback Ed.)
     1. Dwarf planets—Juvenile literature. I. Title.
     QB698.C37 2011
     523.49'2—dc22   2009037810

Printed in China

052010 Leo Paper Group, Heshan City, Guangdong, China

10 9 8 7 6 5 4 3 2 1

To Our Readers: We have done our best to make sure all Internet addresses in this book were active and appropriate when we went to press. However, the author and the publisher have no control over and assume no liability for the material available on those Internet sites or on other Web sites they may link to. Any comments or suggestions can be sent by e-mail to comments@enslow.com or to the address on the back cover.

Image Credits: Dr. R. Albrecht, ESA/ESO Space Telescope European Coordinating Facility, NASA, p. 18; Eliot Young (SwRI) et al., NASA, p. 15; IAU/Robert Hurt (SSC), p. 38; International Astronomical Union/Martin Kornmesser, pp. 4–5; Johns Hopkins University Applied Physics Laboratory/Southwest Research Institute (JHUAPL/SwRI), p. 41; Lowell Observatory Archives/JHUAPL, p. 11; Lunar and Planetary Institute, pp. 14, 16; NASA, pp. 7, 37 (top), 42 (top); NASA and G. Bacon (Space Telescope Science Institute), p. 9; NASA, ESA, and G. Bacon (STScI), p. 21; NASA, ESA, and A. Feild (STScI), p. 39; NASA, ESA, and Adolph Schaller (for STScI), pp. 3, 30; NASA, ESA, and M. Brown (California Institute of Technology), p. 35; NASA, ESA, H. Weaver (JHU/APL), A. Stern (SwRI), and the HST Pluto Companion Search Team, p. 20; NASA/Johns Hopkins University Applied Physics Laboratory/Southwest Research Institute, pp. 23, 24, 42 (bottom); NASA/JPL, p. 33; R. Hurt (SSC-Caltech), JPL-Caltech, NASA, pp. 1, 37 (bottom); Samuel Oschin Telescope, Palomar Observatory, p. 34.

Cover Image: R. Hurt (SSC-Caltech), JPL-Caltech, NASA

Cover illustration shows dwarf planet Makemake and a hypothetical moon.

CONTENTS

INTRODUCTION

Mercury Venus Earth Mars Jupiter

THE eight planets and five dwarf planets of our solar system are shown. Note that sizes are to scale, but distances from the Sun are not.

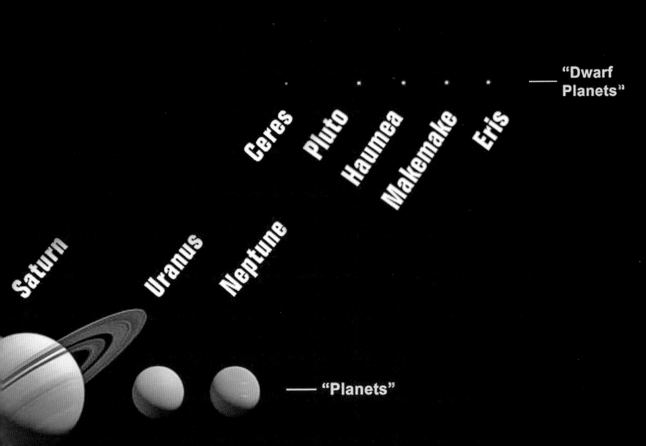

Ceres Pluto Haumea Makemake Eris — "Dwarf Planets"

Saturn Uranus Neptune — "Planets"

Pluto gets so cold that sometimes its air freezes and falls as snow. Wow! How do we know this? Scientists use special telescopes to see Pluto's atmosphere. You will learn lots more far-out facts about Pluto and other icy worlds in this book. Just keep reading!

Pluto was once called the ninth planet. In 2006, scientists switched Pluto to a new category called dwarf planets. Neptune may now be the outermost regular planet, but it is not the last stop in the solar system. Dwarf planets like Pluto are still fascinating worlds—just small ones.

OTHER PLACES LIKE PLUTO

While Pluto is no longer the ninth planet, it is also no longer alone. Astronomers have discovered more worlds very much like Pluto. As telescopes have improved, these faraway worlds out past Pluto have come into view. It is like seeing a city from far away. At first you see only skyscrapers. But as you zoom in with binoculars, all sorts of buildings begin to appear. The more you look, the more you see. The more astronomers look, the more they find.

One of the newly found dwarf planets, called Eris, is a bit bigger than Pluto. Another, called Haumea (how-MAY-ah), is oval-shaped and has two tiny moons. Dwarf planet Makemake (MAH-kay-MAH-kay) is reddish and has no known moons. Pluto and these other fascinating icy dwarf planets orbit out on the edge of the solar system. They are in the Kuiper belt, a ring of rocky hunks of ice out past Neptune.

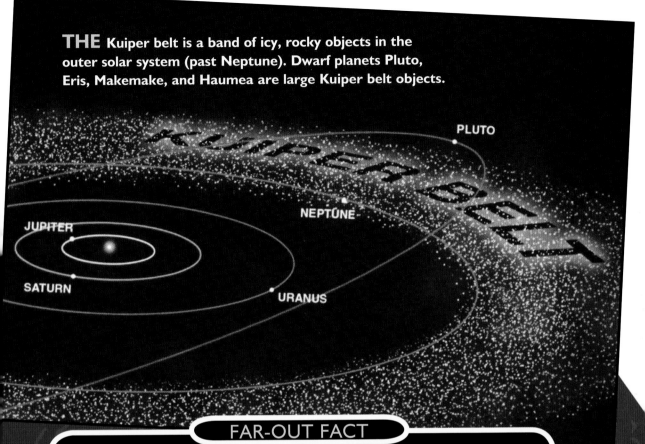

THE Kuiper belt is a band of icy, rocky objects in the outer solar system (past Neptune). Dwarf planets Pluto, Eris, Makemake, and Haumea are large Kuiper belt objects.

PLUTO

NEPTUNE

JUPITER

SATURN

URANUS

KUIPER BELT

CERES STANDS ALONE

All the dwarf planets, except Ceres, are Kuiper belt objects. Ceres is instead an asteroid, orbiting with other asteroids between Mars and Jupiter. At nearly 1,000 kilometers (605 miles) across, Ceres is the biggest asteroid by far. But it is the smallest dwarf planet. When Giuseppe Piazzi discovered Ceres in 1801, he called it a planet. But as other rocky worlds were found near Ceres, it became the largest member of a newly created group of objects called asteroids. In 2006, big round Ceres was reclassified as a dwarf planet.

★

Many Kuiper belt objects (KBOs) are small, but others are large. The largest KBOs are dwarf planets. Pluto is a member of a large family of cold, icy KBO worlds.

FAR-OUT FACT

WHAT IS A DWARF PLANET?

Dwarf planets share characteristics with the eight regular planets. Planets and dwarf planets orbit the Sun, are not moons, and are big enough to be round. Gravity pushes all big objects—stars, planets, moons—into round balls, or spheres. Why? Gravity pulls all objects in toward their centers. Planets and stars have a lot of gravity. It squashes them into the only shape in which every part is pulled in as close to the center as possible—a sphere. So how are dwarf planets different from the eight regular planets? Dwarf planets are surrounded by other small objects similar to themselves. Their paths around the Sun are crowded with objects like asteroids or hunks of ice. The gravity of very large objects, such as regular planets, sweeps their paths clear of other similar objects. So far, astronomers have named five dwarf planets: Pluto, Eris, Makemake, Haumea, and Ceres.

THIS is an illustration of a Kuiper belt object. Scientists believe there could be 100 billion Kuiper belt objects (KBOs) larger than a kilometer (0.6 mile) wide.

CHAPTER I

From Planet X to KBO King

In 1928, a Kansas farm kid named Clyde Tombaugh sent a letter to a famous observatory. The twenty-two-year-old put his drawings of Mars and Jupiter in the envelope, too. Tombaugh had drawn the pictures of the planets while looking through his homemade telescope. The letter impressed the observatory's director—so much that he offered the young man a job. Tombaugh jumped at the opportunity to work for the Lowell Observatory in Arizona. Becoming an astronomer would be a dream come true.

SEARCHING FOR PLANET X

Clyde Tombaugh's job at the observatory was to look for a planet out past Neptune. Astronomers had been looking for this so-called Planet X since

CLYDE Tombaugh was a twenty-four-year-old amateur astronomer when he discovered Pluto in 1930.

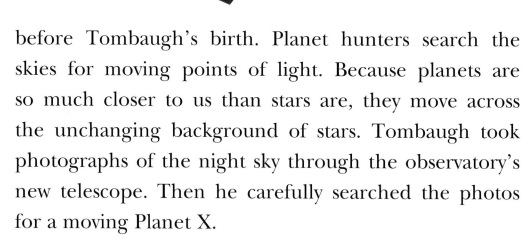

LOWELL'S QUEST

In 1905, an astronomer named Percival Lowell (1855–1916) thought he noticed something odd about the orbit of Neptune. He believed that the gravity of an unknown ninth planet— Planet X—was causing it. Lowell spent the final years of his life searching for Planet X at the observatory he founded in Flagstaff, Arizona. He never found it. The symbol astronomers use for Pluto includes P and L, the first two letters of Pluto and the initials of Percival Lowell.

before Tombaugh's birth. Planet hunters search the skies for moving points of light. Because planets are so much closer to us than stars are, they move across the unchanging background of stars. Tombaugh took photographs of the night sky through the observatory's new telescope. Then he carefully searched the photos for a moving Planet X.

On February 18, 1930, Tombaugh was comparing different photographs of the same patch of night sky taken days apart. The background stars were in the constellation of Gemini. Where all the white dots stayed in the same place in the photographs, Tombaugh knew there was no planet. But then he saw a dot of light shift its place from one photograph to another. The white speck moved a little to the left in the later photograph. It was a planet far past Neptune. Clyde Tombaugh went and found his boss. "I have found your Planet X," he said.

FAR-OUT FACT

PLUTO'S YOUNG DISCOVERER

Clyde Tombaugh (1906–1997) had never been to college when he arrived at Lowell Observatory. He had lived and worked on a farm with his parents and five brothers and sisters. Most of what he knew about astronomy he had taught himself. He had even built his own telescopes. After discovering Pluto, Tombaugh received college scholarships and became a professional astronomer. He later discovered fourteen asteroids and two comets.

AN ODD ORBIT

Pluto's path around the Sun, or orbit, is not like the eight planets'. Think of the orbits of the planets as marbles rolling around in circles on a table. They all move along the same plane—the table. Pluto's orbit is like a squashed hula-hoop shoved through the table at an angle. This angled skinny oval orbit causes Pluto to cross over inside Neptune's orbit. For 20 years of Pluto's 248-year journey around the Sun, Neptune is farther from the Sun than Pluto is.

NOTICE Pluto's orbit. It takes the dwarf planet inside Neptune's path during part of its journey around the Sun.

Neptune

Pluto

Tombaugh's discovery was front-page news around the world. When an eleven-year-old English girl heard about it, she suggested the name Pluto. Pluto is the ancient Roman god of the dark underworld.

A computer made this map of Pluto's surface from images taken by the *Hubble Space Telescope.* Astronomers are not sure why Pluto is darker brown around its equator.

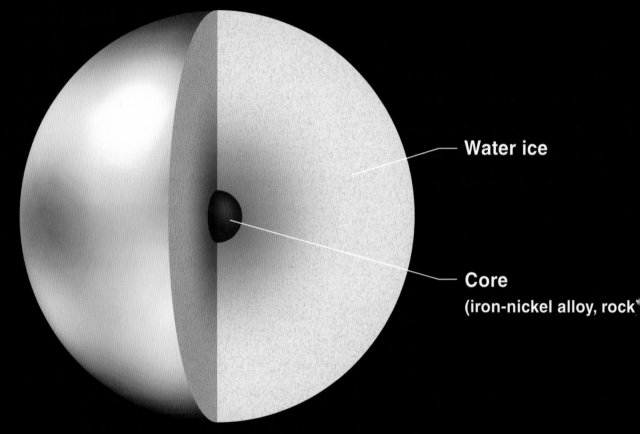

PLUTO likely has a solid
rocky center surrounded by
water ice that's topped with a
covering of frozen methane.

Water ice

Core
(iron-nickel alloy, rock)

PLUTO

A SHRINKING MISFIT

When Claude Tombaugh discovered Pluto in 1930, everyone called it a planet. Lowell Observatory astronomers at first thought that Pluto was larger than *planet* Earth. And astronomers had been looking for a *Planet* X. What else could Pluto be but a *planet?* As astronomers learned more about Pluto over the years, they realized it was small and less planet-like than they had thought.

Studying such a distant, small place like Pluto is difficult. Not much was known about Pluto until space telescopes and satellites started getting a clearer view of it. Even today, the best pictures we have of Pluto show only a fuzzy, faraway world. So what do astronomers know about Pluto? It is small and not very heavy. Pluto is smaller than Earth's moon, and its width would not span the continental United States. Six Plutos would weigh about as much as the Moon. Pluto is also cold and dark.

If you stood on Pluto, the daytime Sun would look like a star in the twilight sky. Pluto is 30 times farther

THE Hubble Space Telescope took this
picture of Pluto and Charon from 4.4 billion
kilometers (2.7 billion miles) away.

Charon

Pluto

PARTNER PLANETS

In 1978, astronomers discovered Pluto's large moon
Charon. Charon is about half Pluto's size and is covered
in water ice. Pluto and Charon are locked in an orbit that
keeps each one facing the other as they travel around the
Sun. No moon is so near the size of the object it orbits as
Charon. This makes Pluto and Charon a binary system, or
double planet. If you stood on Pluto and looked at Charon,
it would never move across the sky like our moon does.
Pluto would look as if it were hovering in place if you
looked at it from Charon.

from the Sun than Earth. If you looked around on Pluto, you would see rock-like hunks of ice everywhere. Pluto's surface is made of gases like nitrogen and methane frozen into ices harder than stone. The ices on Pluto evaporate into space when it orbits closer to the Sun. When it is farther from the Sun, Pluto's thin atmosphere freezes and falls as snow.

KBO KING

The more astronomers learned about Pluto, the less it fit in with the eight planets. It is too icy to be a terrestrial planet like Mercury, Venus, Earth, and Mars. Nor is it a gas giant like Jupiter, Saturn, Uranus, and Neptune. Its orbit is very different from those of the other planets, too. Some started to ask: Is Pluto really a planet? If so, what kind of planet is it?

In the 1990s, astronomers began finding other places like Pluto. They discovered icy worlds out past Neptune that have odd Pluto-like orbits. Some were binary systems, and many had tiny moons. Sound familiar? Astronomers located these Pluto-like worlds in the newly discovered Kuiper belt. Pluto's long-lost

ASTRONOMERS using the *Hubble Space Telescope* discovered two tiny new moons around Pluto in 2005. Nix and Hydra are between two and three times farther from Pluto than its big moon, Charon.

Pluto

Nix

Hydra

Charon

family members were finally found—Kuiper belt objects. And giant KBO Pluto seemed to be their king. Since Pluto was the biggest known KBO, some still considered Pluto a planet. But the discovery of an even bigger KBO—Eris—changed Pluto's standing in the solar system.

THIS illustration shows what the Pluto system might look like from the surface of Hydra or Nix, Pluto's two tiny moons. Pluto is on the left, and Charon is on the right.

PLUTO and ERIS
AT A GLANCE

PLUTO

Diameter: 2,302 kilometers (1,430 miles)

Mass: About .0022 Earth, or 13,000,000,000 trillion kilograms

Gravity: 75-pound kid would weigh 6 pounds

Average Distance from Sun: 5.9 billion kilometers (3.7 billion miles)

Day Length: 153 hours 18 minutes

Year Length: 248 Earth years

Color: Light brown

Atmosphere: Methane, nitrogen, and carbon monoxide

Surface: Ices

Minimum/Maximum Surface Temperature: –233/–223° Celsius (–387/–369° Fahrenheit)

Moons: 3

Namesake: Roman god of the underworld

Discovery Date: 1930

ERIS

Diameter: About 2,400 kilometers (1,490 miles)

Mass: About .0028 Earth, or 16,700,000,000 trillion kilograms

Gravity: 75-pound kid would weigh 8 pounds

Average Distance from Sun: 10.2 billion kilometers
(6.3 billion miles)
Day Length: 7 hours 12 minutes
Year Length: 557 Earth years
Color: Yellowish gray
Atmosphere: Probably nitrogen and methane
Surface: Ices
Minimum/Maximum Surface Temperature: −243/−218°
Celsius (−406/−360° Fahrenheit)
Moons: 1
Namesake: Greek goddess of discord and strife
Discovery Date: 2003 (identified in 2005)

Dysnomia

Namaka

Charon

Hi'iaka

Eris

Pluto

MAKEMAKE and HAUMEA
AT A GLANCE

MAKEMAKE

Diameter: About 1,500 kilometers (932 miles)
Mass: About .0007 Earth, or 4,000,000,000 trillion kilograms
Gravity: 75-pound kid would weigh 5 pounds
Average Distance from Sun: 6.85 billion kilometers (4.3 billion miles)
Day Length: Unknown
Year Length: 308 Earth years
Color: Red-brown

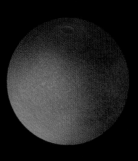

Makemake

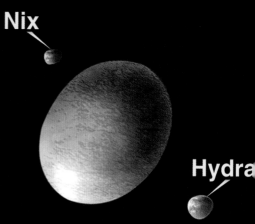

Nix

Hydra

Haumea

Atmosphere: Unknown

Surface: Ices

Surface Temperature: −243° Celsius (−406° Fahrenheit)

Moons: None known

Namesake: Creator of humanity and fertility god in the mythology of Easter Island's Rapa Nui people

Discovery Date: 2005

HAUMEA

Dimensions: 1,960 long x 1,518 wide x 996 kilometers thick (1,218 x 943 x 619 miles)

Mass: About .0007, Earth or 4,200,000,000 trillion kilograms

Gravity: 75-pound kid would weigh 4½ pounds

Average Distance from Sun: 6.4 billion kilometers (4 billion miles)

Day Length: 3 hours 55 minutes

Year Length: 285 Earth years

Color: Gray

Atmosphere: Unknown

Surface: Water ice–covered rock

Surface Temperature: −241° Celsius (−402° Fahrenheit)

Moons: 2

Namesake: Goddess of childbirth and fertility in Hawaiian mythology

Discovery Date: 2004

ICY DWARF PLANETS

ICY DWARF PLANET FACTS

★ A dwarf planet is an object that orbits the Sun, is large enough for gravity to force it into a sphere, has other similar objects in its orbital neighborhood, and is not a moon.

★ The International Astronomical Union (IAU) created the dwarf planet category in 2006 when it wrote a definition of *planet* that did not include Pluto.

★ There are five dwarf planets in all. The giant asteroid Ceres is a *rocky* dwarf planet. Pluto, Haumea, Makemake, and Eris are small *icy* dwarf planets with thin atmospheres.

★ Frost on the surface of some icy dwarf planets melts and puffs up like steam into an atmosphere when their orbits bring them closer to the Sun. When they are farther from the Sun, the air refreezes and falls as snow or forms frost.

★ Haumea, Makemake, and Eris were all discovered within a four-month period between late 2004 and early 2005.

★ Icy dwarf planets are in the Kuiper belt, a region of icy objects out past Neptune. As Kuiper belt objects (KBOs) themselves, icy dwarf planets share their orbits with lots of other KBOs.

★ Gerard Kuiper predicted that the Kuiper belt existed in the 1950s, forty years before a KBO was discovered.

★ A number of the moons of Uranus and Neptune, including Neptune's moon Triton, are likely KBO escapees.

FAST FACTS ABOUT ICY DWARF PLANETS
★

PLUTO FACTS

★ The Sun is so far from Pluto that it looks like a bright star in Pluto's always twilight sky.

★ So little sunlight reaches Pluto that during its winter, its air freezes and falls as snow.

★ Pluto's surface is made of solid rock-like ices.

★ Living on Pluto would mean giving up yearly birthdays. It takes 90,553 Earth days for a year to pass on Pluto.

★ Pluto spins in the opposite direction of Earth. On Pluto, the Sun rises in the west and sets in the east.

★ Its largest moon, Charon, is about half Pluto's size, while Nix and Hydra are tiny moons.

★ Pluto's thin atmosphere is mostly nitrogen gas, with some carbon monoxide and methane.

ERIS FACTS

★ Eris is the largest dwarf planet and the largest known KBO.

★ Eris is the largest Sun-orbiting world discovered since Neptune in 1846.

★ While Eris is only about 5 percent wider than Pluto, it has 28 percent more mass.

★ Eris is the most distant object seen, so far, in orbit of our sun.

★ Eris's single small moon, Dysnomia, is about one-eighth its diameter.

★ Eris reflects much more light than Pluto. Scientists do not know why Eris is so bright.

★ Images of Eris were first recorded by a robotic telescope in 2003, but the dwarf planet was not identified until 2005.

MAKEMAKE FACTS

★ Makemake is the third largest dwarf planet and is about two-thirds the size of Pluto.

★ Its frozen methane surface has a reddish color.

★ Makemake is so far the only known icy dwarf planet without a moon.

★ It is a bit farther out, dimmer, and colder than Pluto.

★ Makemake was given a name from the mythology of the people of Easter Island because it was discovered at Easter time.

HAUMEA FACTS

★ Haumea is round enough to be a dwarf planet, but it is not a perfect sphere. It is shaped like a somewhat flattened egg. (That is why it has three dimensions.) Its widest part is twice as wide as its narrowest.

★ The two tiny moons Namaka and Hi'iaka orbit Haumea.

★ Haumea has about one-third as much mass as Pluto.

★ Scientists think that Haumea may have been created when two KBOs crashed into each other. The crash tore off the icy top layer and left mostly rock. It also could have created the two moons and set the remaining KBO spinning so fast that it stretched it out into its odd egg shape.

★ Haumea has the fastest spin of any known object its size in the solar system.

★ Haumea's long, thin, oval orbit seems unstable. Scientists think that it could become a comet in a billion years or so.

★ The name was chosen because the Hawaiian goddess Haumea represents the element of stone, and this icy dwarf planet is unusually stony.

Icy Dwarf Planets Timeline
of Exploration and Discovery

1905—Percival Lowell begins searching for Planet X beyond Neptune.

1930—Clyde Tombaugh discovers Pluto.

1950s—Gerard Kuiper describes the Kuiper belt.

1978—James Christy and Robert Harrington discover Pluto's large moon Charon.

1988—Astronomers discover Pluto's thin atmosphere.

1992—David Jewitt and Jane Luu discover the first Kuiper belt object.

1994—*Hubble Space Telescope* creates the first map of Pluto's surface.

2004—Mike Brown, Chad Trujillo, and David Rabinowitz discover Haumea and its two moons.

2005—Mike Brown's team discovers Eris and its moon, and they later discover Makemake.

Astronomers discover two small moons circling Pluto: Nix and Hydra.

2006—The International Astronomical Union (IAU) redefines *planet*; Pluto, Eris, and Ceres are declared dwarf planets.

Space probe *New Horizons* launches. It will become the first spacecraft to reach Pluto in 2015 and the Kuiper belt in 2016.

2008—IAU creates class of icy dwarf planets (called plutoids) that includes Pluto, Eris, and newly named dwarf planets Makemake and Haumea.

THIS illustration shows dwarf planet Eris and its tiny moon, Dysnomia. The faraway Sun is the brightest star to the right.

CHAPTER 2

Finding Eris, the Goddess of Troublemaking

Mike Brown was raised on space stuff. He grew up hearing the rumble of rockets at the nearby space-flight center where his dad worked. The rumblings made the poster of the planets on his wall shake just a little. Years later, astronomer Mike Brown really shook up that planet poster.

A TENTH PLANET?

It all started in 1998. That was the year Mike Brown and his team of astronomers started looking for really big Kuiper belt objects (KBOs). "[W]e wanted to see if there was something bigger than Pluto out there," says Brown. Their planet-hunting method was a lot like Clyde Tombaugh's—just higher tech. "Clyde

FROM IDEA TO OBJECTS

In the 1950s, famous astronomer Gerard Kuiper wrote about the possibility of a ring of small objects out past Neptune. No telescope at the time was powerful enough to see if he was right. In 1992, the first known object in just such a place was found. Astronomers named the region the Kuiper belt in his honor. Since then, astronomers have identified thousands of Kuiper belt objects (KBOs).

Tombaugh . . . would take two photographic plates and compare them and look for something that moves," explains Brown. "We now use digital cameras instead and the computer does most of the work that Clyde Tombaugh did." The robotic telescope Brown's team used is also nearly four times as big as Tombaugh's and can see much fainter objects.

Seven years after starting their search, Brown was at work flipping through pictures of the night sky on his computer. The robotic telescope had taken the pictures in 2003. "Suddenly this big bright object appears on my screen," said Brown. At first he did not believe what he

Uranus, Neptune and Pluto

In 1986 Voyager 2 revealed the true nature of Uranus (top left), which lays on its side between the orbits of Saturn and Neptune. Uranus has a bevy of narrow rings and astounding moons. Since 1993 JPL's Wide-Field and Planetary Camera (WFPC2) on NASA's Hubble Space Telescope has continued to observe Uranus.

In 1989 Voyager 2 sped past Neptune (top right), discovering narrow rings and many small satellites. Neptune is the windiest planet, with winds blowing at speeds over 2,400 kilometers (1,500 miles) per hour.

Distant Pluto and its moon Charon— 30 to 50 times farther from the Sun than Earth is— have not been visited by spacecraft. The European Space Agency's Faint Camera on NASA's Hubble Space Telescope provided this view (bottom).

ASTRONOMER Mike Brown and his team discovered the dwarf planet Eris in 2005. It is the largest object discovered orbiting the Sun since Neptune's discovery in 1846.

saw, so he checked twice to make sure the object he was seeing was really there. "I did a very quick calculation, and I realized it was bigger than Pluto," he said. The astronomer immediately picked up the phone. He called his wife and told her, "Hey, I just found a planet!"

The "planet" that Brown and his team had discovered was later named Eris. It is a dark, cold KBO three times as far from the Sun as Pluto is. "It's five percent bigger than Pluto," says Brown. "It's probably made out of the same materials—rock on the inside, ice on the outside, and a little thin layer of frost on the very outside that sometimes puffs up into an atmosphere and sometimes

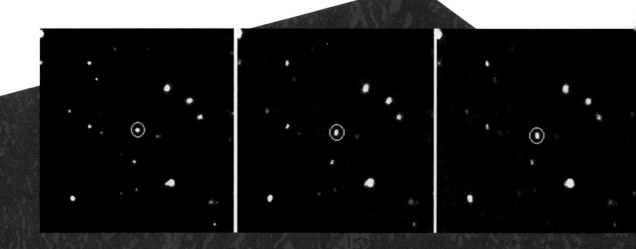

THESE pictures show how Eris was discovered. It shows a circled Eris moving slightly across the background of stars.

THIS image of Eris and its moon Dysnomia was taken by the *Hubble Space Telescope* in 2006.

doesn't, very similar to Pluto in that way." A moon called Dysnomia orbits Eris once every sixteen to seventeen days. Brown sees Eris as Pluto's twin in some ways. "This is just the twin that ate a little more when it was a baby and got a little bigger."

A DWARF PLANET

In 2005, Mike Brown and his team announced that they had found the tenth planet. Since at the time Pluto was the ninth planet, Eris *was* the tenth—right? Many astronomers did not agree. Eris is a KBO, they argued, not a planet! But then Pluto would have to be a KBO, too. If Eris was not a planet, how could smaller Pluto be a planet? And if Eris was the tenth planet, what about the other big round KBOs? Mike Brown's team had discovered several of those. Were they planets, too? It was a fierce debate. In Greek mythology, Eris is a troublemaking war goddess. Eris sure earned its name!

The scientific organization in charge of naming planets, moons, and other solar system objects decided to settle the argument. In 2006, the International Astronomical Union (IAU) decided that Eris was *not* the tenth planet. And Pluto was not the ninth planet, either. The solar system has only eight planets. The IAU invented a new category for Pluto, Eris, and other small worlds—dwarf planets. Pluto, Eris, and the once-asteroid Ceres were immediately declared dwarf planets.

How did Mike Brown feel about it? "I'm of course disappointed that [Eris] will not be the tenth planet," he told reporters in 2006. But he felt the IAU did the right thing for astronomy. "Pluto would never be considered a planet if it were discovered today," he said. New discoveries change what we know. And new knowledge can change what a word means and how we use it—like the word *planet.* In 2008, two more of the big round KBOs discovered by Mike Brown's team joined the dwarf planet club. Makemake is a reddish world a bit smaller than

HAUMEA was the fifth named dwarf planet, and the oddest world yet. It is oval-shaped and tumbles end over end every four hours, making it one of the fastest spinning objects in the solar system.

DWARF planet Makemake is likely covered in reddish frozen methane. Its name is pronounced MAH-kay-MAH-kay. Makemake is the creator of humanity and the fertility god of the mythology of Easter Island's Rapa Nui people.

WHAT *IS* A PLANET?

The original meaning of *planet* was "wanderer," after the objects that moved across the night sky. For ancient peoples, the planets included the Sun and the Moon. After astronomers discovered that planets orbit the Sun, the meaning changed. Now that we know about worlds like Pluto and Eris, the meaning of *planet* has changed again. The IAU defines a planet as a round object that orbits the Sun along a path free and clear of other objects like itself.

MEMBERS of the International Astronomical Union voted on a new definition of *planet* in 2006 that did not include Pluto.

Pluto. Haumea is a fast-spinning egg-shaped KBO with two moons. Scientists will learn a lot more about dwarf planets and KBOs in the coming years. Right now a spacecraft is on its way to the Kuiper belt and Pluto.

FAR-OUT FACT

PLUTOIDS

As discoveries of dwarf planets beyond Neptune started to pile up, the IAU decided to give them their own group name. They called them plutoids, a class of dwarf planets. Like all dwarf planets, plutoids are round objects that orbit the Sun in a neighborhood not cleared of other objects. For a dwarf planet to be a plutoid, it must orbit out past Neptune. So far, class plutoid includes Pluto, Makemake, Eris, and Haumea. If astronomers decide to keep the name, other newly discovered Pluto-like worlds may be called plutoids someday.

Dysnomia — Eris

Namaka / Charon / Hi'iaka — Pluto

Makemake

Nix / Hydra — Haumea

CHAPTER 3

What's Next for Pluto-like Worlds?

No spacecraft has visited Pluto or the Kuiper belt so far. Telescopes have taught scientists what we know about these icy worlds. *New Horizons* may change that. Launched in 2006, the robotic space probe is now racing toward Pluto at a speed of more than 1.5 million kilometers (1 million miles) per day. Scientists will likely learn more about Pluto during *New Horizons*'s short visit than in the eighty years since it was discovered.

Alan Stern is the scientist in charge of the *New Horizons* mission. Watching Apollo astronauts land on the Moon as a kid got Stern hooked on space. "I just got real excited by the Apollo program and wanted to be a part of space exploration," says Stern. Now Stern is getting ready to explore the mysterious worlds of the Kuiper belt. Pluto and the other icy Kuiper belt objects are ancient leftovers from the early solar system. "So by traveling through the Kuiper belt, we will have a chance to unravel that history like an archaeological dig back into the history of our solar system," says Stern.

EXPECT SURPRISES

New Horizons is the fastest spacecraft ever launched. It reached the Moon in only six hours. (It took Apollo astronauts a couple of days to reach the Moon.) Even at this breakneck speed, the journey to Pluto will take nine years. *New Horizons* is set to arrive at Pluto in July of 2015. The spacecraft will get closer

THIS illustration shows the *New Horizons* spacecraft arriving at Pluto in 2015. What would you like it to find out about Pluto and the Kuiper belt?

ENGINEERS get *New Horizons* ready for its 2006 launch.

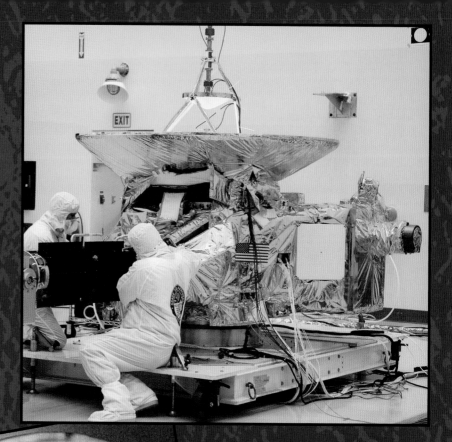

THIS small canister is attached to *New Horizons*. Inside are some of the ashes of Pluto's discoverer, Clyde Tombaugh.

INTERNED HEREIN ARE REMAINS OF AMERICAN CLYDE W. TOMBAUGH, DISCOVERER OF PLUTO AND THE SOLAR SYSTEM'S " THIRD ZONE." ADELLE AND MURON'S BOY, PATRICIA'S HUSBAND, ANNETTE AND ALDEN'S FATHER, ASTRONOMER, TEACHER, PUNSTER, AND FRIEND: CLYDE W. TOMBAUGH (1906-1997)

and closer until it can see features the size of football fields. Instruments and cameras on board will take pictures and study Pluto's atmosphere and surface. The spacecraft will also fly by Charon and Pluto's other moons. After leaving the Pluto system, *New Horizons* plans to fly by and study one or two smaller Kuiper belt objects.

What will *New Horizons* find on Pluto and in the Kuiper belt? Stern says to "expect the unexpected." The space probe might find underground oceans or geysers on Pluto. "It's a whole new kind of world," says Stern. "It's a planet I think everyone has tried to imagine." Stern looks forward to finally finding out what Pluto is really like. Stern says, "It'll be worth the wait, and then some."

FAR-OUT FACT

DAWN TO DWARF PLANET CERES

Remember Ceres, the only rocky (not icy) dwarf planet? A spacecraft is also on its way to visit this gigantic asteroid. *Dawn* was launched toward the asteroid belt in 2007. If it reaches Ceres as planned in 2015, it will be the first mission to a dwarf planet. *Dawn* will photograph and study Ceres. The space probe's instruments will try to figure out what its surface is made of, and also what lies underneath.

★

Words to Know

Apollo—Space program of the 1960s and 1970s that sent the first humans to the Moon's surface.

asteroid—A large rock that orbits the Sun.

asteroid belt—The region of space between Mars and Jupiter where most asteroids are found.

atmosphere—The gases that are held by gravity around a planet, moon, or other object in space.

binary system—Two objects in space that orbit each other.

comet—A large chunk of frozen gases, ice, and dust that orbits the Sun.

double planet—Out-of-date term for a binary system.

dwarf planet—A round space object that orbits the Sun and shares its orbit with other similar objects.

gas giant—A planet made of mostly gas and liquid and no land, including Neptune, Saturn, Uranus, and Neptune.

gravity—An attractive force on one object from another.

International Astronomical Union (IAU)—The scientific group that names planets, moons, and other space objects.

Kuiper belt—A band of billions of ice and rock chunks past Neptune's orbit.

Kuiper belt object (KBO)—An object in the Kuiper belt.

mass—The amount of matter in something.

methane—Natural gas, or a gas made of a specific combination of carbon and hydrogen.

WORDS TO KNOW

★

moon—An object in space that naturally orbits a larger object in space.

NASA—The National Aeronautics and Space Administration, the space agency of the United States.

observatory—A place with telescopes and other instruments for observing planets, stars, and other objects.

orbit—The path followed by a planet, moon, or other object in space around another object; to move around an object in space.

planet—A large, sphere-shaped object in space that is alone (except for its moons) in its orbit around a sun.

satellite—An object that orbits a larger object, such as a moon or a machine launched into space that orbits Earth.

space probe—A robotic spacecraft launched into space to collect information.

space telescope—A telescope that orbits Earth or travels in space.

sphere—A ball or globe; a shape whose surface points are an equal distance from the center.

terrestrial planet—A rocky solid planet with a metal center, including Mercury, Venus, Earth, and Mars.

year—The time it takes for an object in space to travel once around the Sun.

Find Out More and Get Updates

Books

Bourgeois, Paulette. *The Jumbo Book of Space.* **Toronto: Kids Can Press, 2007.**

Fraknoi, Andrew. *Wonderful World of Space.* **New York: Disney Publishing, 2007.**

Rusch, Elizabeth. *The Planet Hunter: How Astronomer Mike Brown's Search for the 10th Planet Shook Up the Solar System.* **Flagstaff, Ariz.: Rising Moon, 2007.**

Scott, Elaine. *When Is a Planet Not a Planet?* **Boston: Clarion, 2007.**

Vogt, Gregory L. *Pluto: A Dwarf Planet.* **Minneapolis: Lerner Publications, 2010.**

Other Books by Mary Kay Carson

Exploring the Solar System: A History with 22 Activities. **Chicago: Chicago Review Press, 2008.**

Extreme Planets! Q & A. **New York: HarperCollins, 2008.**

Solar System Web Sites

Johns Hopkins University Applied Physics Laboratory.
   "What We Know About Pluto, Charon and the Kuiper Belt." 2007.
   <http://pluto.jhuapl.edu/science/whatWeKnow.html>

NASA. "Solar System Exploration: Kids." 2008.
   <http://solarsystem.nasa.gov/kids>

University Corporation for Atmospheric Research (UCAR).
   "Windows to the Universe." 2009.
    <http://www.windows.ucar.edu/>
   Click on "Our Solar System." Then click on "Dwarf Planets."

Pluto Explorations Web Sites

Johns Hopkins University Applied Physics Laboratory.
   "New Horizons: Education."
    <http://pluto.jhuapl.edu/education/index.php>

Pluto and Eris Movies

Johns Hopkins University Applied Physics Laboratory.
   "New Horizons: Animation."
   <http://pluto.jhuapl.edu/gallery/animations.php>

Johns Hopkins University Applied Physics Laboratory.
   "New Horizons: Passport to Pluto."
   <http://pluto.jhuapl.edu/gallery/videos/passToPluto.php>

Index